THE BOOK OF
CAMOUFLAGE
The Art of Disappearing

OSPREY
PUBLISHING

First published in Great Britain in 2013 by Osprey Publishing,
Midland House, West Way, Botley, Oxford, OX2 0PH, UK
44-02 23rd Street, Suite 219, Long Island City, NY 11101, USA
E-mail: info@ospreypublishing.com

Osprey Publishing is part of the Osprey Group

A CIP catalogue record for this book is available from the British Library

ISBN: 978 1 78200 831 6
E-pub ISBN: 978 1 4728 0293 4
PDF ISBN: 978 1 4728 0292 7

Typeset in Perpetua
Originated by PDQ Digital Media Solutions, UK
Printed in China through Asia Pacific Offset Limited

13 14 15 16 17 18 10 9 8 7 6 5 4 3 2 1

Osprey Publishing is supporting the Woodland Trust, the UK's leading woodland conservation charity, by
funding the dedication of trees.

www.ospreypublishing.com

Editor's note: All images are © Private Collection, Peter Newark's Pictures.

THE BOOK OF
CAMOUFLAGE
The Art of Disappearing

TIM NEWARK

The very first camouflage was used by hunters to disguise themselves from their prey and could take the form of foliage or mud smeared over their bodies, to hide their scent as well as their appearance. In this scene, portrayed by artist George Catlin in 1840, North American Plains Indians creep up on grazing buffalo while wearing wolf skins; the Native Americans hope their skin covering imbues them with the spirit of the predator animal so that they can scatter and separate the buffalo just as a pack of wolves might. Hunters today continue to use camouflage, wearing both camouflage pattern textiles and the more traditional ghillie suit, which was devised by Scottish gamekeepers and made up of hundreds of strips of cloth attached to netting. The ghillie suit is a favourite with army snipers too. More recently, hunter Bill Jordan founded the Realtree camouflage company in 1986 which produces very effective textile designs of overlaying leaves, twigs and bark that create a three dimensional illusion of foliage.

British Army riflemen of the early 19th century. A soldier of the 60th (Royal American) Foot stands, while one from the 95th Rifle Regiment kneels. Both were members of elite regiments that engaged in a new kind of warfare – skirmishing – which saw them advance in open formation, using cover, to shoot at closely ordered ranks of brightly uniformed soldiers. They deployed the more accurate rifle – rather than the musket – and wore green jackets to camouflage their movements. They were the predecessors of the modern combat soldier, and the 95th has since been made famous by the *Sharpe* novels of Bernard Cornwell. The artist of this illustration was Captain Charles Hamilton Smith, who served in the 60th and was an accomplished natural historian. He once carried out an experiment to determine which was the most effective uniform colour to camouflage a soldier at a distance and concluded that grey was more effective than green – the colour worn by the Austrian sharpshooting *Jager*.

The Corps of Guides, a combination of cavalry and infantry raised by Henry Lumsden in the Punjab in 1846, was the first unit in the British Army to wear khaki. Khaki is a Hindi word meaning dust-coloured, derived from the Persian *khak* for soil or dirt. Lumdsen equipped his native soldiers with loose-fitting trousers and jackets based on the local *kurta*, which he then had dyed with river mud that produced more of a grey, rather than brown, colour. Major William Hodson, second-in-command of the Corps of Guides realized its camouflage value when he said the khaki uniforms made his soldiers 'invisible in a land of dust'. Ten years later, during the Indian Mutiny, British soldiers improvised khaki uniforms by dyeing lightweight white clothing with tea or curry powder. It was a temporary measure, however, and abandoned soon after, much to the relief of British colonists, one of whom declared, on seeing a column of khaki-clad British soldiers, that they were 'dreadful looking men'.

A colour-sergeant and a private of the Gloucester Regiment demonstrate the two styles of British Army uniform worn in 1900. Just four years earlier khaki had been accepted into the British Army for all overseas service; it was worn at the battle of Omdurman and during the Boer War. In 1902 it became the official uniform colour for home service too, making the much-loved scarlet jacket purely ceremonial dress. In the same year, khaki also became the official combat outfit for the US Army. Experiments with camouflage patterns painted on coastal gun emplacements were carried out during the late Victorian era, both in the UK and abroad. A War Office report of 1886 on defences in Malta said that 'if the concrete was coloured and the guns distempered, the battery would be hard to make out'. Another report described coastal forts in the UK 'painted in broad reds, greens and yellows'. It would take a world war, however, to truly introduce the world to the importance of military camouflage.

A British howitzer painted with a camouflage pattern on the Western Front. Camouflage first appeared on the battlefield in World War I as a way of protecting large military weaponry from aerial observation. Netting and tarpaulins were pulled over artillery to obscure the view from early reconnaissance aircraft searching for gun positions to report back to enemy artillery batteries. Green and brown paint was also used to disguise this weaponry, taking the lead from khaki soldiers, so they would merge into the landscape. As aerial photography was in black and white, however, the colour was less important than the ability to break up the telltale silhouette of weapons. This was best achieved through painting barrels with contrasting stripes of light and dark colours. It was the first use of disruptive patterning in warfare and can be seen clearly in this photograph.

A French military camouflage artist – a *camoufleur* – paints the barrel of an artillery piece. The French were the first to realize the value of camouflage in World War I and, from 1915, deployed artists in painting units attached to their armies in the field. Parisian portraitist Lucien-Victor de Scevola was the leading figure in this development and was rapidly promoted from private to captain as he oversaw a small army of nearly 10,000 men and women painting weaponry in workshops along the Western Front. Throughout the combat, however, he maintained the pose of a successful artist and was observed to dress as a dandy with white kid gloves. Several prominent French artists served alongside him and at least 15 were killed. The word camouflage is of French origins and is believed to stem back to the 17th century, when *camouflet* was used to describe a puff of smoke blown into the face of someone to confuse or blind them. However, *camoufler* can also mean to make up for the stage.

A British field gun being painted with camouflage and disguised with netting. Slower to adopt camouflage than the French, it was not until 1916 that the British established their own camouflage section. Commanded by Lieutenant-Colonel Francis Wyatt of the Royal Engineers, it too turned to professional artists for their visual expertise. Among them was Solomon J. Solomon, who strongly argued the case for camouflage, saying that 'the side which neglects it will be unduly exposed to the onslaught of an adversary who will be concealed, and whose whereabouts cannot be detected'. Working alongside Solomon were other successful artists, including Ernest Shepard, who later became famous for his illustrations that accompanied A.A. Milne's *Winnie the Pooh*. Solomon's camouflage unit was known as the Special Works Park and was based with the Royal Engineers at Wimereux in France, where it ran several workshops to create camouflage materials, including painted canvases and netting.

German *stahlhelm* painted with disruptive pattern camouflage. This steel helmet, introduced for German combat troops from 1916 onwards, was the only item of camouflage worn by the German Army in World War I and was a favourite with trench-assaulting 'storm-troopers'. The idea did not spread to uniform textiles – it would take another 20 years before the Germans pioneered that. In the meantime, Germans did use camouflage to hide artillery positions and, like the Allies, recruited artists for their expertise. Franz Marc, an Expressionist artist, painted tarpaulins for artillery positions, but let his artistic sensibilities run wild, producing a set of patterns in the style of famous artists 'from Manet to Kandinsky'. The Germans understood that it was the disruptive pattern that mattered and not the colours, so eschewed a muddy palette when it came to covering aircraft and enjoyed decorating them with brightly coloured polygonal patterns.

British troops in roughly dug trenches await the signal to attack during the Third Battle of Ypres in October 1917. They have painted their helmets with light splodges to create an improvised form of disruptive patterning. Personal camouflage for British troops in World War I was mainly restricted to sniper outfits. This could take the form of canvas smocks and mittens hand painted with dark and light brown and green paints, plus black stripes and some attached foliage. It was only in March 1918 that two sniper suits officially went into production for use in the British Army: one was a boiler suit with a hood of scrim – loosely woven fabric for attaching foliage – and the other was the Symien sniper suit made entirely of scrim, with separate leggings, rifle cover and gloves. White snow suits and a dark overall for use at night were also developed, but the war came to an end before any further advances in camouflage clothing were made by the British.

French designs for sniper and reconnaissance suits incorporating disruptive patterning. Although they pioneered the use of camouflage in World War I, the French were slow to adapt it to military clothing. Their infantrymen even entered the war in brightly coloured red trousers before casualty rates forced them to switch to their characteristic 'horizon blue' combat uniform. It was left to Eugene Corbin to experiment with camouflage clothing at Nancy. Around 1916, he produced an elegant tunic and waistcoat in green with hand-splattered blue spots. He also designed similarly camouflaged sniper overalls, but none of these went into production. The British were more open to these experiments, but even a complex Op-Art style geometric design hand painted in oils by Percyval Tudor-Hart on sniper gloves was deemed too avant-garde by the War Office in 1917 and no better than simpler, hunter inspired outfits.

Page from the French booklet *La Guerre et les Artistes*, showing how steel observation posts can be camouflaged on the battlefield. Such metal tubes could be disguised to look like shell-blasted tree stumps and erected on the battlefield at night. Sometimes a real tree stump was chopped down and then replaced by a fake one that looked exactly the same. Other observation posts were placed inside a false water-filled crater or a dummy dead horse. More elaborate camouflage schemes were devised to hide entire artillery batteries, including vast swathes of netting that conformed to the boundaries of a real field. The Germans were even more ambitious, developing 'Strategic Camouflage' to hide buildings or entire units by using gently sloping camouflage materials so that the artificial structures left no shadows at all.

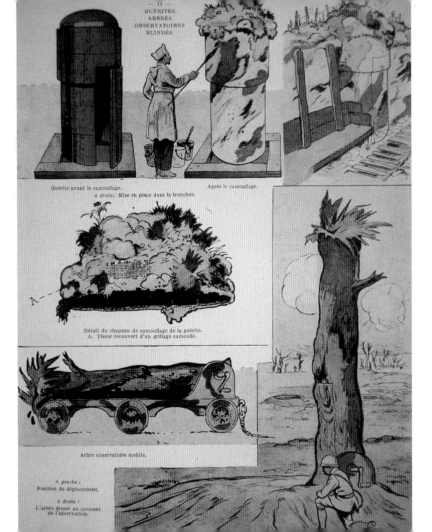

Guérite avant le camouflage.

Après le camouflage.

à droite: Mise en place dans la tranchée.

Détail du chapeau de camouflage de la guérite.
A. Viseur recouvert d'un grillage camouflé.

Arbre observatoire mobile.

à gauche:
Position de déplacement.

à droite:
L'arbre dressé au moment
de l'observation.

Camouflaged British Mk IV tank in action against a German tank, illustration published in *The Sphere*, August 1918. From 1916, when tanks first crawled on to the Western Front, they were prime candidates for disruptive pattern camouflage. Some war artists were inspired by their appearance, such as C.R.W. Nevinson who portrayed a tank in 1917 painted with green, black and red stripes. British tanks were painted in a single colour on the production line and only painted with camouflage patterns on the battlefield. The same was true of Germans tanks, which emerged from factories painted in a variety of shades of field grey. Camouflage was only widely adopted on German tanks at the time of their Spring Offensive in 1918, most of this being random splodges of contrasting colours, but some later schemes appear to be more formalized with patches of ochre, red-brown and dark green separated by black lines, similar to *stahlhelm* patterning.

British Royal Navy cruiser painted with a camouflage scheme sails through the Dardanelles in 1915. Unlike static artillery positions that could be camouflaged to merge with their landscape, battleships were large objects moving against an ever-changing seascape. Disruptive patterning was therefore the best form of naval camouflage, helping to break up the profile of a ship. Lieutenant-Commander Norman Wilkinson, a marine artist, took this concept a step further when he devised 'dazzle camouflage', an extravagant form of disruptive patterning. Based on his own sailing experience, he knew that shades of grey or blue were not effective enough. Seeing it from the point of view of the submarine commander, the camouflage pattern had to distort the very shape and progress of the vessel; 'The primary object of this scheme … was not so much to cause the enemy to miss his shot when actually in firing position, but to mislead him, when the ship was first sighted, as to the correct position to take up … consequently making it a matter of difficulty for a submarine to decide on the exact course of the vessel to be attacked.'

Ship covered in dazzle camouflage in dry dock in Liverpool, painted by Edward Wadsworth. Not only was the modernist artist Wadsworth inspired by the surreal sight of these ships to create some of the most striking art of World War I, he was also recruited by Wilkinson to help oversee the application of the patterns at Bristol and Liverpool. Numerous others artists were employed at the Royal Academy of Art to test the best schemes on little wooden models, which were then viewed through a periscope. 'The colours mostly in use,' recorded Wilkinson, 'were black, white, blue and green, either in their primary condition, or mixed to various tones. When making a design for a vessel, vertical lines were largely avoided. Sloping lines, curves and stripes are by far the best and give the greater distortion.' Dazzle was mainly used on merchant vessels, not battleships, as it could do little to protect from shelling by enemy warships. It was designed primarily to disrupt the activity of German U-Boats attacking convoys bringing food and supplies to Britain.

Rare photograph showing a dazzle-painted British merchant vessel sinking, after being struck by a torpedo in 1917. Dazzle was not a magic shield, as this photograph clearly shows, but there was some evidence to indicate that it did help reduce the number of merchant ships sunk during the war. 'The dark painted stripes on her after part made her stern appear her bow,' noted one naval commander, 'and a broad cut of green paint amidships looks like a patch of water. The weather was bright and visibility good; this was the best camouflage I have ever seen.' The US Navy took up dazzle and by the end of the war had over 1,200 merchant vessels covered in the scheme, claiming that less than one per cent of them had been sunk by enemy torpedoes. The British Admiralty, however, set up its own investigation and found there was no concrete proof that U-Boat commanders had been confused by the patterning, concluding that its primary purpose was to raise the morale of their merchant seaman who believed that the system offered them some protection.

Party-goer wearing a costume designed for the Dazzle Ball in 1919, celebrating the end of World War I. It is perhaps the very first example of camouflage being worn as civilian fashion. Held at the Royal Albert Hall, the Dazzle Ball was hosted by the Chelsea Arts Club and art students made their own costumes inspired by Norman Wilkinson's naval designs. 'The very fact that this disruptive colouration broke up the usual lines of form gave to many of the costumes a grace and charm as delightful as they were unexpected,' wrote the *Times* correspondent at the party. 'Even the freakish creations held the suggestion of a new kind of wonder, the "camouflage" of men and women.' With a jazz band playing in the background, these revellers were seen to be expressing a new spirit that wanted to escape the dark days of the war and dedicate itself to enjoyment. Camouflage, it seemed, had become 'cool' and so began an association with counter-culture that would grow in the later part of the century.

Italian camouflage tent issued in 1929 – the first recorded use of printed camouflage textiles. With the end of World War I, the need for camouflage came abruptly to an end. It was very much viewed as a battlefield measure that had no place in armies devoted to the maintenance of peace. That said, the impact of camouflage patterns continued to intrigue artists and an American painter, H. Legard Towel, conducted experiments with fellow artists into the best forms of natural camouflage painted on loose-fitting clothing. In France, a detailed illustrated essay exploring the various applications of camouflage appeared in *La Guerre Documentee*, published in Paris around 1920. It showed soldiers clad in hooded overalls painted with bold disruptive patterns. In the land that gave birth to Futurism, it is perhaps no surprise that the Italian Army should follow up on such experimentation and produce camouflage tents. The pattern chosen for it has proved an enduring one, being revived for the Italian Army in 1992.

German oak leaf pattern in green spring colouration. The very first camouflage uniforms produced with printed textiles were devised in Germany in the 1930s. They were developed within the Waffen-SS, the paramilitary arm of the Nazi party, by SS-Sturmbannführer Wim Brandt, a doctor of engineering and commander of a reconnaissance section, and Professor Otto Schick. Apparently, artists had first been approached by the Waffen-SS, but Brandt preferred the nature-inspired patterns of Schick. Taking as his inspiration the appearance of bark peeling off plane trees and light filtering though the leafy foliage of an oak tree, he produced three main patterns, later termed oak leaf (*Eichenlaubmuster*), plane tree (*Platanenmuster*) and palm tree (*Palmenmuster*). The patterns chimed perfectly with the pagan culture of the SS and traditional German affinity with the forest, and were in contrast to the angular shapes of the *Splitter* (splinter) camouflage pattern adopted by the German Army, thus drawing a clear line between the two military forces.

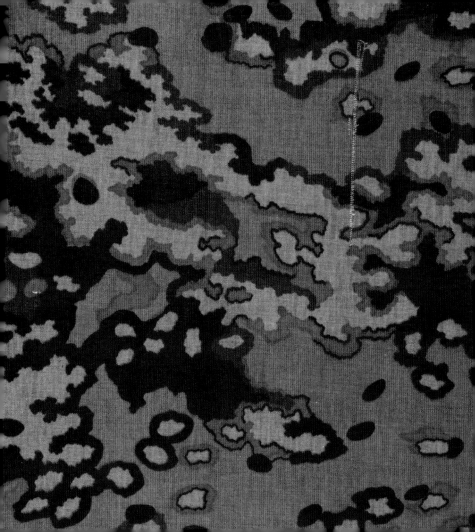

German oak leaf pattern in brown autumn colouration. Brandt and Schick's tree camouflage patterns were tested in 1937 during Waffen-SS manoeuvres and were found to reduce casualties by some 15 per cent. They went into production shortly afterwards as a helmet cover and pullover smock, both being printed with a reversible pattern of spring green and autumn brown so the same item could be worn in different landscapes at different times of year. A Reich Patent was awarded to Schick for this use of his patterns, which ensured that they could not be adopted by the German Army but remained the distinctive pattern of the Waffen-SS. At first the textiles were produced by laborious hand screen-printing, but by 1940 the process was speeded up with the introduction of roller press printing, resulting in the delivery of 33,000 camouflaged smocks to Waffen-SS units. By 1944, the smock was superseded by a camouflage drill uniform with tunic and trousers.

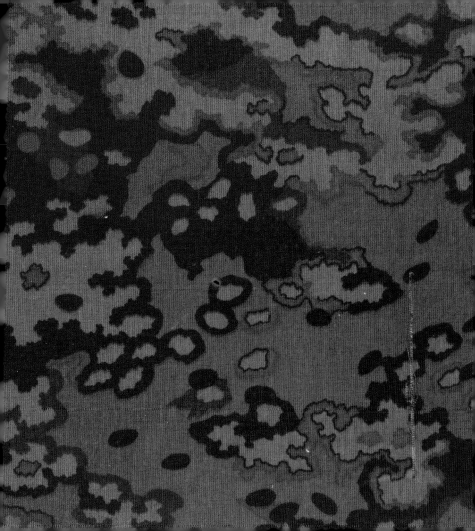

Waffen-SS cavalrymen in Russia during World War II, part of a brigade formed in August 1941, pictured wearing camouflage smocks. At the end of the war an American military report, authored by Francis S. Richardson, QMC Consultant, described the progress of Waffen-SS camouflage patterns. 'As first conceived the printed design had sharp, distinct lines between colours,' noted Richardson. 'Later this was altered so the lines were less distinct and the edges of each colour were irregular and tended to shade off.' This tendency continued throughout the war until 'this pattern was again modified so as to produce an even more blurred effect or blending from one colour to another'. Seen at a distance, the green/brown patterns tended to merge together, so a new motif – reinforcing the effect of disruptive patterning – was developed with strongly contrasting black shapes. Called *Leibermuster*, it was to be worn by all German troops in 1945, but the collapse of the Third Reich meant it never reached the battlefield.

German *Zeltbahn* in oak leaf pattern. The *Zeltbahn* was a triangular waterproof sheet that could either be attached to other sheets to form a tent or used by itself as a poncho, wind break or stretcher. It was the very first item to be ordered in camouflage for the German Army in June 1930, and appeared the following year, reflecting the influence of the Italian Army's camouflage tent. The first pattern chosen for the *Zeltbahn* was the *Splitter* motif consisting of jagged shapes overlaid by green broken lines or a 'falling rain' pattern that became the standard camouflage of the Wehrmacht. In 1943, a variant of this pattern appeared in which the edges of the angular shapes were blurred; this became known as the *Sumpfmuster* or swamp pattern. The Waffen-SS produced its own distinct camouflaged *Zeltbahn* from 1939 to 1944.

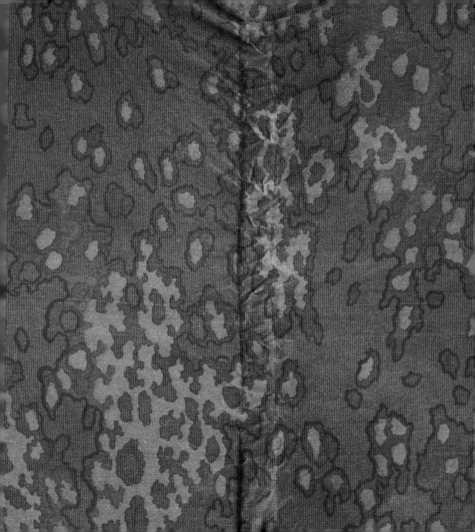

Sleeve of German camouflaged smock, showing detail of *Palmenmuster* or palm tree pattern. This was one of the more literal tree patterns developed by the Waffen-SS but had nothing to do with palms. Bunches of feather-like leaves can be seen on the sleeve, perhaps inspired by studying ash trees, while radiating darks lines on the shoulders led it to be called 'tiger shirt' by troops. Spots and furry blobs on the back may represent fruits or seed pods. IG Farben manufactured the dyes used in Waffen-SS patterns that not only worked as camouflage in normal lighting conditions but also when viewed through infrared sights. Richardson, in his US Army report, made a detailed study of the various chemical dyes used and the complicated processes involved, at one point taking photographs of the various patterns through an infrared filter. The later *Leibermuster* textiles can be seen to have an even stronger disruptive patterning effect seen through the infrared lens.

German combat trousers featuring the *Erbsenmuster* or pea pattern. This evolved out of the oak leaf pattern and appeared in 1944 with the issue of two-piece camouflage uniforms. It was not reversible and combined green and brown colouration. The predominance of camouflage outfits worn by German soldiers during the Normandy campaign and afterwards is said to have discouraged the US Army in the European theatre from issuing its own troops with camouflage clothing developed in the Pacific War, as it was thought to be too confusing and could result in friendly fire incidents. Certainly Richardson concluded his study of German camouflage uniforms in 1945 with some doubts as to their usefulness; 'Whether the results justified the effort is difficult to determine,' he wrote. 'Talks with US Army combat officers would seem to bear out the fact that camouflage does not help if the object is in motion, be it a tank or man.' Such a comment, however, failed to acknowledge the value of disruptive patterning, which was not even mentioned in his report.

Three versions of camouflaged sniper suits designed for use by the British Home Guard in the event of an invasion of Britain by the Germans in World War II. Left to right: painted boiler suit, overcoat suit and suit made out of hessian sacking with painted disruptive pattern. From Roland Penrose's *Home Guard Manual of Camouflage,* 1941. Before the war, Penrose was a noted surrealist artist who introduced Salvador Dali to the London art world. Volunteering his services to the Home Guard, he nevertheless maintained his surrealist sensibilities as many of his camouflage designs reveal. They also had to be produced on the cheap and sometimes this went too far, as when he instructed rural aircraft spotters to smear their faces with locally sourced materials. 'By some who live in country districts,' he advised, 'cow-dung has been advocated and for those who have the courage to use it, it can be highly recommended in spite of its unpleasantness, since it retains good colour and texture when dry.'

Detail of British camouflaged Denison smock. Although the British realized the value of camouflage for protecting buildings from aerial attack and large vehicles on the battlefield in World War II, they were slow to apply it to soldiers' uniforms, preferring instead their traditional khaki. In 1941, however, the Denison smock was developed for use by airborne forces. Designed by Captain Denison, who had served in a camouflage unit led by Oliver Messel, a noted stage designer, the waterproof item was covered with a pattern that owed something to its artistic genesis, as the motifs look as though they have been painted on with a brush. This pattern was later resurrected in the classic brush-stroke DPM (Disruptive Pattern Material) worn by the British Army from the 1960s. Camouflage jackets were also worn by commando and SAS units in World War II and, largely remaining the property of British Special Forces, did not transfer to the ordinary infantryman.

Punch cartoon of April 1940 showing British seamen trying to camouflage themselves as 'rivets' by painting their steel helmets grey. Humour was used throughout World War II in official British publications to encourage the use of camouflage both by the military and civilian population. The art editor of *Punch* at the time was also the cartoonist Cyril Kenneth Bird, who illustrated an instructional booklet called *Hide & Seek* for the government. In it, Bird tells a story in rhyming couplets about two brothers, Albert and Thomas Hide, who like their smart uniforms and don't wish to cover them up: 'Now many people by and large, look down their nose at camouflage. "S'all right for those who can, perhaps, but not for ordinary chaps, half magic, half a boring trick – bad form – a nuisance – makes me sick."' But it is the bright shiny buttons on Albert Hide's uniform that attract the German bomb that kills his brother Tom. A harsh lesson, but part of the government's determination to spread the use of camouflage.

Experimental US Army camouflaged uniforms photographed at Fort Ethan in Vermont in 1942. Like the British, the Americans first entered World War II with a one-colour khaki uniform, but this was quickly switched to their characteristic olive drab. Experiments in camouflage, however, had been conducted by the US Army's Corps of Engineers since 1940. A winning design was produced by Norvell Gillespie, a gardening editor for *Better Homes and Gardens,* which was dubbed 'frog-skin' pattern, as it imitated a natural amphibian camouflage of rounded shapes in green and brown. Like German forest patterns, it was produced in a reversible version of mainly green and mainly brown colouring – beach and jungle – and this became the primary form of camouflage worn by US forces in World War II. Experiments continued throughout the war, including a desert pattern uniform of black stripes contrasted against pale browns, a little like the *Leibermuster* developed by the Germans towards the end of the war.

1st US Marine Raiders demonstrate a river crossing by ropes at Camp Allard, New Caledonia, March 1943. The first camouflage uniform issued to the Marines was a one-piece overall, but this was unpopular with soldiers serving in a hot climate, especially if suffering from loose bowels, and they had to cut their own bottom flaps into it. The overall was replaced by a two-piece uniform, as shown in the photograph. The US Marine Raiders were an elite unit specializing in amphibious warfare, trained in landing in fast inflatable boats and operating behind enemy lines. Lieutenant-Colonel Merritt Edson commanded the first battalion and they became known as 'Edson's Raiders'. Hand-picked from volunteers, the Marine Raiders were given the best equipment, which included camouflage outfits, reinforcing the association of camouflage with Special Forces in World War II. They saw action in the Guadalcanal campaign in the central Pacific, but by 1944 the development of amphibious tractors and improved fire support for beach landings meant there was no longer any need for specialized assault units and the Raiders were disbanded.

US Marine flame-thrower operator wears camouflage combat suit and has his face smeared with camouflage face cream. Never very popular in the Pacific theatre, camouflage uniforms were not worn by US forces in Europe following the Normandy campaign, partly because of their similarity to Waffen-SS camouflage and largely because US officers felt they made moving soldiers more of a target than their usual olive drab. The concept of disruptive patterning was not fully appreciated and the wearing of camouflage combat uniforms among American forces had already started to decline from 1943. The camouflage helmet cover, however, was popular and continued to be worn by the US Army after the war until the 1960s. Taking inspiration from the German *Zeltbahn*, a camouflage shelter-half and poncho were issued, while Marine paratroopers were given a camouflage smock.

Infantry of US 1st Division wearing white bed sheets as improvised snow camouflage for their advance to the front near Faymonville, during the Battle of the Bulge, January 1945. Specialized white camouflage winter and mountain warfare clothing was issued to elite units in the US Army, but not in any great numbers and not on the battlefield. When US soldiers had to fight the German surprise winter offensive in the Ardennes, they had no choice but to make their own helmet covers and ponchos cut out of sheets and tablecloths. A general shortage of experienced fighting men among the Allies from 1944–45 meant that special terrain units could not be maintained and soldiers were reallocated throughout the army with standard GI issue equipment. German and Soviet forces made greater use of winter camouflage, but they too were hindered by equipment shortages towards the end of the war.

Soviet women snipers wearing camouflage combat suits. The first camouflage worn by Soviet forces, as with other armies in World War II, was reserved for specialized units such as snipers, reconnaissance and paratroopers. It took the form of a 'jigsaw' pattern, as seen in the photograph, which became characteristic of Soviet forces during and immediately after the war: so much so that Warsaw Pact troops from Eastern Europe in the Cold War era often wore jigsaw-derived patterns to underline their alliance with the Soviet Union. First introduced in 1938, the Russian jigsaw pattern was later joined by a delicate 'twigs and leaves' pattern in 1941. Because it was produced in such large quantities, the twigs and leaves pattern continued to be worn by some Soviet forces into the 1960s and surplus material was donated to Romania, where it was worn in to the 1990s. A jagged leaf pattern entered Soviet service in 1944 and can be seen to be the first version of what would later become the widely worn 'pixel' motif.

Czech camouflage pattern from the 1950s. This seems to combine two influences, the Soviet 'jigsaw' pattern with the German experimental urban pattern, *Leibermuster*. Czechoslovakia was a major centre for German war production during World War II and it is claimed that the machinery for producing camouflage textiles had been shifted there during the final stages of the war. This may well have influenced a series of Czech military patterns immediately after the war, which copy German *Splitter* patterns along with its 'falling rain' motif. The red and black of this pattern is often mistaken for a rare surviving example of the *Leibermuster*. It was worn by Czech airborne troops from the 1950s to the 1970s. During World War II, volunteer Czech troops fighting with the Allies in airborne units wore Denison smocks, which is hardly surprising as many of them were trained by the British. Immediately after the war, Czech airborne units wore Denison smocks made out of the Italian 1929 tent pattern.

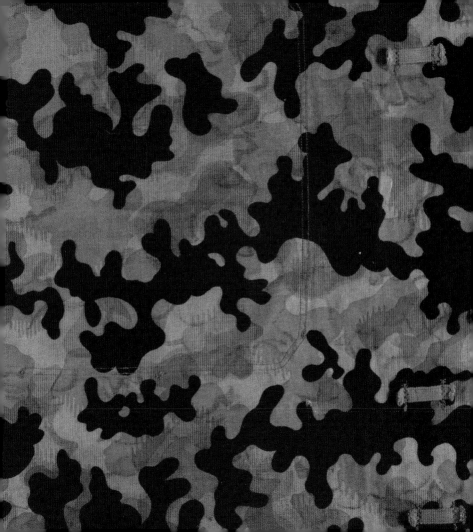

Polish camouflage pattern from the 1970s. Like its Czech neighbour, Polish camouflage came under the influence of the Soviet-led Eastern Bloc and adopted both 'jigsaw' and 'twigs and leaves' patterns. A strong German influence was evident too in its *Splitter* patterns and the 'falling rain' motif, which by itself later became characteristic of Warsaw Pact forces from the 1950s onwards. By the 1970s, however, the Polish Army was showing signs of independence in its camouflage design when it chose a leopard skin motif for its Special Forces. Wrongly supposed to express an African influence, this choice is much more likely to have been inspired by the leopard skin cloaks worn by elite Polish troops from an earlier period in the 17th century – the Polish Winged Hussars – who were, in turn, influenced by Turkish cavalry warriors clad in animal skins and feathers as a sign of their 'hunter' profile on the battlefield. Other animal-inspired patterns, including tiger stripe and frog skin, were also developed in the Polish Army. Now completely free of Soviet dominance, Polish camouflage shows a more Western influence.

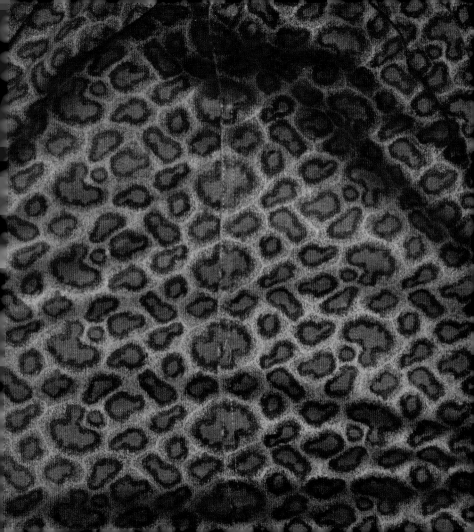

Finnish camouflage pattern of the 1960s. The Finns first encountered camouflage during the Russo-Finnish War at the beginning of World War II, when their country was invaded by opportunist Soviet forces. Soviet leader Joseph Stalin believed he would have an easy victory over the smaller nation, but his lack of success against the Finns later encouraged Adolf Hitler and the German Army to invade the Soviet Union. During this bitter war, the Finns wore white snowsuits, matching those worn by the Russians. Avoiding Soviet or Western influence after the war, the Finns developed their own distinctive pattern in the 1960s, which stayed largely unchanged until the early 21st century. It was produced in several different colour schemes, which may have reflected changing seasons and was nicknamed 'cucumber salad' by the Finns. Harking back to the country's wartime experience, most of these patterned uniforms were reversible to white.

Swiss camouflage pattern of the 1960s. Famously neutral since the 19th century, the Swiss have one of the most distinctive camouflage patterns, owing to its use of red, perhaps reflecting the colour of its national flag. The camouflage was widely used in combat trousers worn by young people in the 1990s and was a key pattern in the development of camouflage as a popular street style. And yet the pattern has a strong wartime origin – looking very similar to the German *Leibermuster* developed towards the end of World War II, which featured both black and red colouring in its urban pattern. Some claim that it arrived in Switzerland via Czechoslovakia, who provided wartime camouflage textile machines. Certainly, the very first Swiss camouflage patterns worn from 1938 onwards were directly copied from German *Splitter* patterns. The Swiss *Leibermuster* pattern evolved in the late 1950s and continued in service into the 1990s. It has since been replaced by a more typically military-looking pattern of green and browns, though maintaining the vein of black, but sadly without the popular red.

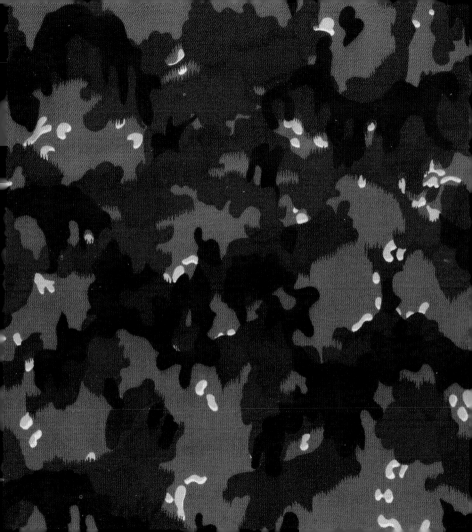

Danish camouflage pattern of the 1980s. This distinctive Danish pattern shows the strong influence of the German forest-inspired motifs of the 1930s, with two shades of green and a black that sometimes look purple. Brown was supposedly left out of the mix because the flat Danish landscape has little rocky terrain, but it may also have been to distance it from any German wartime models. Straight after World War II, the Danish Army was equipped with British uniforms and this included some camouflaged clothing. It was not until the late 1970s that the Danes began to develop their own national camouflage pattern. This entered service in 1984 and was later produced in a desert version, being worn by its United Nations peacekeeping forces in the Horn of Africa, Iraq and Afghanistan. A completely different US-originated camouflage was introduced in 2011, doing away with the attractive Danish landscape pattern.

Zaire camouflage pattern of the 1970s. The African Republic of Zaire, now known as the Democratic Republic of Congo, was formerly part of the Belgian Congo and the influence of its colonial past can be seen in much of its camouflage. Belgian 'brushstroke' patterns, ultimately deriving from Britain, and Belgian 'jigsaw' patterns both feature among the military clothing worn by Zairean forces, but in the 1970s the elite soldiers of its Kamanyola Division began to wear a purely African leopard skin design. However, even this may owe its origin to a Belgian manufacturer and similar patterns have been worn in Chad and Libya. Just as Soviet-influenced camouflage was worn widely by Warsaw Pact troops, so the camouflage worn in African countries can frequently be traced back to its colonial past or an influential Cold War patron.

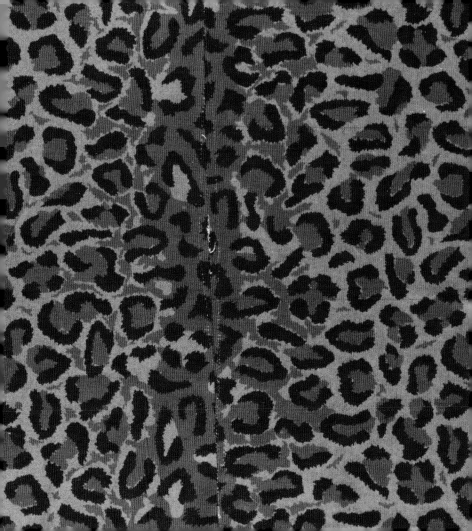

French Foreign Legion paratrooper armed with an MAT 49 machine gun in North Africa in 1965. He wears the distinctive French 'lizard' pattern camouflage. In fact, it is more of 'brushstroke' pattern, referring back to the painterly origin of French and British camouflage in World War I. After World War II, camouflage was first worn by French paratroopers during their colonial war in Indo-China from 1953 onwards. It consisted of three colours with the broad brushstrokes of green and brown feathering off into streaks against the fabric background. The fighting in South-East Asia ended with defeat at Dien Bien Phu, but paratroopers continued to wear this pattern during the French colonial war in Algeria. Algerian insurgents learned to avoid camouflage-wearing units as they would be French elite troops, instead preferring to attack khaki-clad conscripts. Perhaps because camouflage was worn by paratroopers involved in an attempted coup in 1961, camouflage was withdrawn from French troops based at home. It continued to be worn, however, by the French Foreign Legion in the 1960s.

French camouflage pattern of the 1990s. From the 1960s to the 1980s, most French soldiers did not wear camouflage – it had a bad association with defeat in colonial conflicts. Trials with a German-style pattern were dropped in the 1980s precisely because it was too close to wartime forest patterns, but with French involvement in the Gulf War in 1990, a new desert pattern was developed. It became known as the 'Daguet' pattern after Operation *Daguet*, the French equivalent of America's *Desert Storm*. The desert pattern was later followed by a woodland-coloured version for use in Europe and worn during French involvement in Balkan campaigns in Bosnia and Kosovo.

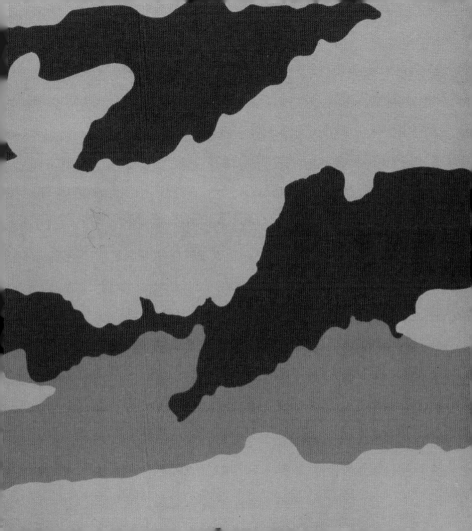

British Disruptive Pattern Material camouflage. Known simply as DPM, the classic 'brushstroke' pattern was derived from the World War II-era Denison smock, which continued to be worn in the British Army into the 1950s. Developed by the Army Personnel Research Establishment at Farnborough in the 1960s, it was first issued to British soldiers in Northern Ireland in 1969, but was only widely worn from 1972 onwards. Since then it has proved an enduring pattern successfully adapted to a variety of environments and copied by many other nations. A richer coloured version of the four-colour pattern was deployed in British tropical combat dress in 1976 and a simpler two-colour version was adapted for wear in desert conditions during the first Gulf War. A so-called urban pattern version utilizing grey, blue, black and white has been produced commercially but was never worn by the army. Any further variations in colouring were often due to slight differences in manufacturing and dyes, but the basic pattern remained the standard British camouflage for over 40 years, until the British Army introduced a new camouflage pattern in 2010.

US Marines on patrol in Vietnam wearing 'vine leaf' pattern helmet covers. After World War II, camouflage went out of fashion in the US Army and only Marine 'frog' pattern helmet covers were worn during the Korean War. In 1953, the US Marine Corps developed a new pattern featuring leaves and twigs, since called 'vine leaf', but it only saw limited use as helmet covers and shelter half sheets. It continued to be worn into the 1960s. Such was the prejudice against camouflage clothing at the time that when a British officer visited the United States to discuss their research into the effectiveness of combat clothing camouflage in 1961, he was told by US Army officers that disruptive patterning had no real advantage over a single colour that merged with the landscape. At a NATO meeting at the same time, the German Army – pioneers of camouflage uniforms, but perhaps under the Cold War influence of the Americans – declared that they too had decided to revert to a single colour for their combat uniforms. Continued fighting in Vietnam, however, would change this attitude to camouflage.

US Special Forces military advisor instructs a South Vietnamese soldier on the use of a grenade launcher during the Vietnam War. Both soldiers wear 'tiger-stripe' camouflage. Because of the lack of official camouflage clothing in the US Army, many American soldiers in the early years of the Vietnam War were forced to improvise their own camouflage. This included buying commercially available versions of the old 'frog' pattern known as 'duck hunter' because of its use by hunters. In the early days of the war, US military advisers were told to wear the same clothing as the South Vietnamese Army, which included their distinctive tiger-stripe pattern. This later became a favourite of US Special Forces troops – conducting behind-the-lines operations – and became a sign of elite troops in South-East Asia. It even acquired a fashionable status, being privately adapted into civilian wear, including dinner jackets and swimming trunks.

Vietnamese camouflage pattern of the 1960s. In 1958, the South Vietnamese Marine Corps wore a pattern they called 'sea wave'. It was a variant of the brushstroke 'lizard' pattern introduced by French troops during their fighting in Indo-China earlier that decade. Versions of this pattern were then produced by manufacturers throughout South-East Asia, but all of them had the striking black stripe, with the result that it became known as 'tiger-stripe' camouflage in the 1960s when adopted by American troops. With the expansion of the South Vietnamese Army during the Vietnam War, elite Ranger battalions were created and they all wore tiger-stripe camouflage. The popular pattern has spread throughout South-East Asian military forces, including Singapore and Thailand.

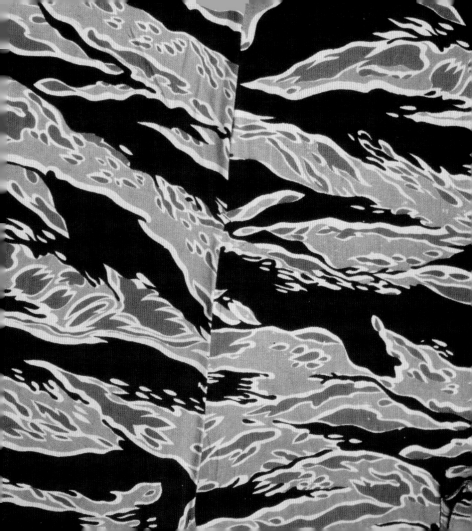

Early version of the US 'woodland' pattern. A new camouflage pattern for the US Army was designed at its Engineering Research & Development Laboratory (ERDL) at Fort Belvoir in Virginia in 1948, but a lack of official interest meant it was shelved until the early 1960s, when the popularity of the 'tiger-stripe' pattern spurred the development of an American tropical camouflage for the Vietnam War. Several hundred combat uniforms printed with the 'ERDL' pattern were sent for evaluation in the jungle fighting and proved popular with Special Forces troops from 1967 onwards, but it was not widely adopted by US armed forces still wary of camouflage. Even the US Air Force preferred its silver skinned jet fighters naked of camouflage, until a 1966 report on the Phantom revealed that the effect of the humid saline atmosphere in South-East Asia on unprotected aluminium alloy was to nearly eat it through. This consequently encouraged the Americans to turn to the British for advice on painting aircraft with camouflage schemes.

US Special Forces on patrol wearing US 'woodland' camouflage. The 'ERDL' pattern saw use in the 1970s, but by the end of the decade scientific research at the US Army Natick Soldier Center produced a new version that worked in both daylight and night vision. The increased use of image intensifiers in night fighting meant that such a pattern had to work in a wide range of spectrums. Research into the comparable effects of dyes and fabrics resulted in the M81 Woodland pattern. 'The light green approximated the appearance of glossy leaves,' explained Richard Cowan of Natick, 'the dark green living foliage, the brown resembled soil and tree trunks, and the black represented shadows and holes in the woods.' It was back to the German forest patterns of the 1930s and, when US troops were seen wearing the pattern during their 1983 invasion of Grenada, a US World War II veteran said, 'I used to shoot at guys who looked like that!' The M81 Woodland camouflage has proved immensely popular and was adopted by numerous other nations for their armed forces – many still wearing it today.

US Army desert camouflage of the 1980s. Research into a desert pattern for US troops began in the 1970s and the result was the classic 'chocolate chip' motif based on the rocky terrain of deserts in the American South-West. It saw widespread use in the 1991 Gulf War and became synonymous with American soldiers in the Middle East, but proved unpopular with US forces and was quickly dropped after the war. Replaced with a simpler, three-colour pattern minus the 'rocky' motif, one of the official reasons for the change was that it had an improved 'psychological effect and is a morale booster'. The fact remains that whatever scientists might think is the best pattern for military camouflage, it still has to win the approval of soldiers on the battlefield and the less 'fancy' a pattern is, the more it is liked. Surplus 'chocolate chip' combat uniforms were passed on to Iraqi troops following the toppling of Saddam Hussein in 2003 and helped to distinguish them from US forces.

CD camouflage covers for the song by rock band Manic Street Preachers about the death of war photojournalist Kevin Carter. Taking two classic patterns – a blue US woodland and a green British DPM – it was designed by Mark Farrow in 1996. Since World War I, artists have been inspired by military camouflage and a magnificent variety of their painterly studies can be seen in the art collection of the Imperial War Museum in London. It was in 1986, however, that artist Andy Warhol introduced the beauty of camouflage to a whole new generation with a massive series of canvases copying the US M81 Woodland pattern in a range of colours. Since then, camouflage has moved from art to design and has grown in popularity as an embellishment for all kinds of objects, from toys to home decoration. 'In Germany the craze is for camouflage bed-sheets,' enthused a newspaper in 2001. 'In France they go wild for camouflaged loo paper while in Belgium camouflage curtains are *all la rage.*'

Camouflage street fashion. During protests against the Vietnam War in the 1970s, some campaigners wore US military camouflage, most notable among them being Vietnam Veterans against the War. Since then, camouflage clothing has become part of a 'radical chic' counter-culture, popular among punks and hip hop bands as well as protestors. By the 1990s, however, it was not so much the 'protest' power of camouflage that appealed to more and more young people, as just the sheer 'cool' of the look. British DPM, US woodland and desert 'chocolate-chip', plus Swiss red *Leibermuster*, proved the most poplar patterns to be worn as jeans or t-shirts. Seeing this growing street appeal encouraged fashion designers to make their own camouflage clothing, and leading among these were Versace, Paul Smith, Valentino and Jean Paul Gautier. Camouflage expert, collector and fashion designer Hardy Blechman invented his own peace motif camouflage for his Maharishi label.

British Army Multi-Terrain Pattern (MTP) camouflage. For the first time in more than 40 years, the British Army has a new camouflage pattern. Introduced in 2010, it was devised for soldiers in Afghanistan moving through different landscapes, including scrubland and desert. Tested in the field by the British Defence Science and Technology Laboratory, it was an alternative to the new MARPAT (Marine Pattern) pixelated patterns introduced into the US Army from 2001. 'The boys are very fashion conscious,' said a British Army spokesman. 'A pixelated pattern just didn't work. And, since it's more about fashion than camouflage at close distances, we took this into account. The British camouflage pattern is like the Mini – it's a design classic.' Interestingly, the new British pattern does share some 'brushstroke' motifs with its DPM predecessor and so continues a camouflage tradition that goes back to World War II. In a similar vein, the Multicam pattern issued to US troops in Afghanistan from 2010, references the old woodland camouflage. Sometimes it's hard to beat the classic patterns!

Las Vegas (Red Rock Canyon) camouflage pattern. Devised for *The Future of Camouflage* exhibition in London in 2003 and Barcelona in 2004, it demonstrates an alternative path for the development of camouflage patterns. Since the collapse of the Soviet Union in 1991, new nations liberated from their old Cold War allegiances have sought to express their national identities by creating new camouflage patterns for their armies. Military camouflage is now a badge of recognition as much as a method of disguise – a new heraldry. Why not apply this to civilian identity as well? Every city, every neighbourhood should have its own camouflage pattern. Taking elements from local culture, landscape and history, a new pattern can be devised for local residents. Each motif is combined within the structure of the disruptive pattern principal, but beyond that they are simply an interpretation of a location. It is the next stage in a century-long process in which the value and beauty of camouflage has been slowly recognized beyond its military purpose.

Further Reading

Blechman, H. (ed.), *DPM – An Encyclopaedia of Camouflage*, London (2004)

Forbes, P., *Dazzled and Deceived*, London (2009)

Goodden, H., *Camouflage and Art*, London (2007)

Latimer, J., *Deception in War*, London (2001)

Newark, T. & Q. Newark, *Brassey's Book of Camouflage*, London (1996)

Newark, T., *The Future of Camouflage*, London (2002)

Newark, T., *Camouflage*, London (2007)

Peterson, D., *Waffen SS Camouflage Uniforms & Post-War Derivatives,* London (1995)

Peterson, D., *Wehrmacht Camouflage Uniforms & Post-War Derivatives*, London (1995)

www.camopedia.org website of the International Camouflage Uniform Society

About the Author

Tim Newark is the author of several critically acclaimed studies of camouflage, including *Brassey's Book of Camouflage*, *The Future of Camouflage* and *Camouflage*, the book that accompanied the Imperial War Museum exhibition. For 17 years the editor of *Military Illustrated*, he is also the author of several military histories, including *Highlander* and *The Fighting Irish*. As scriptwriter and historical consultant, he has worked on seven TV documentary series for the History Channel and BBC Worldwide, and contributes book reviews to the *Financial Times*. Visit his website at www.timnewark.com.